Presented to _____

by _____

on _____

Text © 2004 The Livingstone Corporation. © 2004 Standard Publishing, Cincinnati, Ohio. A division of Standex International Corporation. All rights reserved. Sprout logo is a trademark of Standard Publishing. Printed in China. Project editor: Lindsay Black. Design: Robert Glover. Typesetting: SettingPace.

Produced with the assistance of The Livingstone Corporation (www.LivingstoneCorporation.com). Project author: Emily Malone. Project consultant: Dr. Mary Manz Simon. Project staff: Betsy Todt Schmitt, Dr. Bruce B. Barton, David R. Veerman, and Mary Horner Collins.

Scripture quotations taken from the Holy Bible, New Living Translation, copyright © 1996. Used by permission of Tyndale House Publishers, Inc., Wheaton, Illinois 60189. All rights reserved. New Living Translation and the New Living Translation logo are registered trademarks of Tyndale House Publishers, Inc. NLT is a trademark of Tyndale House Publishers, Inc.

10 09 08 07 06 05 04   9 8 7 6 5 4 3 2 1

ISBN 0-7847-1598-X

On-My-Own Reader
BIBLE

illustrated by Shari Warren

Standard Publishing
cincinnati, ohio

The Bible Is for You!

The Bible is an exciting book, especially when you can read it on your own!

The Bible is God's Word—God's message to us. There are 66 different books in the Bible that were written by 40 different people. Not every book of the Bible was written at the same time, but God guided all the writers. So we can be sure that what the Bible says is exactly what God wants us to know!

The Bible is divided into two parts, the Old Testament and the New Testament. Even though the Bible has two parts, it really has one purpose—to tell everyone God's wonderful plan for all of us.

In the Old Testament you will find exciting stories that show the love and power of God. Everything you will read about really happened. Every event was part of God's plan to prepare his people for the coming of the Savior.

The New Testament tells the rest of the story of God's wonderful plan for us. When the time was just right, God sent his Son, Jesus, to be the Savior of the world. Jesus showed us what God is like and taught us how to live to please God.

How exciting to know that the Bible is a message from God for us! He has watched over this special book from the beginning and kept it safe so that everyone can read it—everyone including you!

Table of Contents

Table of Contents

Table of Contents

God made everything
Genesis 1:1–2:3

In the beginning

God made heaven and earth.

God said, "Let there be light."

God called the light "day."

God called the darkness "night."

That was the first day.

God made the waters

and the sky.

That was the second day.

God made the land and the seas.

God made plants

grow on the land.

That was the third day.

God made the sun

to rule the day.

He made the moon

to rule the night.

He also made the stars.

That was the fourth day.

God made fish for the oceans.

God made birds for the sky.

That was the fifth day.

God made every kind of animal.

Finally God said,

"Let's make people to be like us."

Then God blessed the people.

God created the heavens and the earth.
Genesis 1:1, NLT

He said, "Fill the earth and rule it."

That was the sixth day.

God looked over all he had made

and saw that everything was good.

God finished making everything

in six days.

On the seventh day, God rested.

God made the seventh day holy.

Story based on Genesis 1:1–2:3 as it appears in the New Living Translation®.

Adam and Eve disobey
Genesis 3:1-24

Adam and Eve lived

in the Garden of Eden.

The garden was filled with

many beautiful plants and animals.

The serpent was a clever creature.

One day, the serpent spoke to Eve.

"Did God really tell you

not to eat fruit?"

"Of course we may eat it," Eve said.

"But not fruit from the middle tree.

If we eat that fruit, we will die."

"You will not!" the serpent hissed.

"If you eat it, you will be like God."

The fruit looked fresh and tasty,

and it would make Eve so wise.

The woman ate some fruit.

Then she gave some to Adam.

Suddenly they both knew

that they had no clothes.

They made clothes from fig leaves

and hid when they heard God coming.

God called out, "Where are you?"

Adam said, "I hid because I'm naked."

"Who told you that?" God asked.

"Did you eat fruit

I said not to eat?"

The Lord turns his face against those who do evil.
1 Peter 3:12, NLT

"Yes. Eve gave it to me," Adam said.

God asked Eve, "Why did you do it?"

"The serpent tricked me," she said.

God told the serpent, "You will crawl
on your belly in the dust."

Then God told Adam and Eve,

"You will struggle and sweat for food.

You will die and turn back into dust."

Story based on Genesis 3:1-24 as it appears in the New Living Translation®.

Noah builds a boat
Genesis 6-9

There were many people on the earth

who were doing bad things.

They made God sad.

Only Noah was good and obeyed God.

God told Noah,

"I will send a flood to cover the earth.

Make a large boat out of wood.

Put your family

and two of every animal in the boat.

I will keep you safe."

Noah got in the boat with his family.

The animals came with them.

Two by two, the creatures came in.

For forty days and nights it rained.

Water covered all the mountains.

Everything died that lived on dry land.

But God remembered Noah

and the animals.

The rains stopped,

and the waters slowly went down.

The boat came to rest on a mountain.

Noah sent a dove out to find dry land.

The bird returned with a leaf.

A week later, he sent the dove again.

This time it did not come back.

Noah knew the earth was dry at last!

You [God] . . . will keep me safe.
Psalm 4:8, NLT

God said, "Leave the boat, all of you."

So Noah and his family left the boat.

All the animals came out, two by two.

Then God said,

"I am making a promise.

I will never send

another flood like this.

My rainbow is a sign of my promise."

Story based on Genesis 6–9 as it appears in the New Living Translation®.

The people build a tower
Genesis 11:1-9

At one time

all people spoke the same language

and used the same words.

The people traveled east

and settled on a plain

in the land of Babylonia.

They began to talk about building.

"Come," they said.

"Let's make piles of bricks

and find asphalt to use as mortar.

Let's build a great city

with a tower that reaches to the skies.

The city will show our greatness!

"This will bring us together

and keep us together."

God came down

to see the city and the tower

that the people were building.

"Look what they can do now!" he said.

"What will they

be able to do later?

Nothing will be impossible for them!

Come, let's go down

and give them different languages.

Then they will not be able

to understand each other."

LORD, there is no one like you! For you are great.
Jeremiah 10:6, NLT

In that way,

God scattered people

all over the earth.

That ended the building of the city.

So the city was called Babel

because God confused the people.

He gave them many languages

and scattered them across the earth.

Story based on Genesis 11:1-9 as it appears in the New Living Translation®.

God calls Abram
Genesis 12:1-9

God told Abram,

"Leave your country.

Leave your house

and all your relatives.

Go to the land

that I will show you.

I will give you children

and grandchildren.

I will bless you

and make you famous.

I will make you a blessing to others.

Everyone will be blessed

because of you."

So Abram left

as God had told him.

He took his wife, Sarai.

Abram's nephew, Lot,

went with them.

Abram took all his money

and his animals.

He took all his servants.

They traveled for a long time,

and at last they came to a new land.

The land was called Canaan.

Everyone who was with Abram

camped by an oak tree.

You will be my people.
Leviticus 26:12, NLT

God came to Abram.

God told Abram,

"This land is for your children."

Abram wanted

to remember God's visit.

So Abram built an altar

and worshiped God.

Story based on Genesis 12:1-9 as it appears in the New Living Translation®.

A son is promised
Genesis 15:1-7; 17:1-8

One day God spoke to Abram.

God said, "Do not be afraid, Abram.

I will protect you.

You will have a great reward."

Abram asked God,

"How will you bless me?

You have not given me

any children.

I do not even have a son."

God told Abram,

"You will have your own son.

He will get everything

that I am giving you."

God showed Abram the night sky.

God said, "Look up into the heavens.

Count the stars if you can.

Your children will be like that.

Your family will be too large to count."

Abram believed God,

and God was pleased.

God said, "I am the Lord.

I brought you out of your old town

so I could give you this land.

Always serve me and do what is right.

I will make your children great."

At this, Abram praised God.

You [God] have promised good things to me.
2 Samuel 7:28, NLT

God said, "This is my promise.

You will be a father of many people!

I am changing your name to Abraham.

That means 'father of many.'

I will give you many grandchildren.

They will make up many nations.

Some will even be kings!

This promise will last forever."

Story based on Genesis 15:1-7; 17:1-8 as it appears in the New Living Translation®.

Jacob tricks Esau

Genesis 25:19-34

Isaac was Abraham's son.

Isaac married Rebekah

and asked God to give her a child.

So God gave Rebekah twins.

God told her, "Your sons will fight,

and their children will be enemies."

When the time came,

the twins were born.

The first son was all red and hairy.

They called him Esau.

The other twin was born

holding onto Esau's heel.

They called him Jacob.

Then the boys grew up.

Esau became a good hunter

and liked to be outside.

But Jacob liked to stay at home.

One day Jacob was cooking some stew

while Esau was out hunting.

Esau came home tired and hungry.

He said to Jacob, "I am so hungry!

Give me some of that stew you made."

Jacob replied, "All right,

but trade me your birthright for it."

(A birthright is a special blessing

for the firstborn son.)

Store your treasures in heaven.
Matthew 6:20, NLT

"I am dying of hunger!" said Esau.

"What good is my birthright now?"

Jacob said, "Then say right now
that the birthright is mine."

So Esau gave away his birthright.

Then Jacob gave Esau bread and stew.

Esau ate until he was full.

He did not care about his birthright.

Story based on Genesis 25:19-34 as it appears in the New Living Translation®.

Jacob dreams of heaven
Genesis 28:10-22

Jacob was taking a trip.

When the sun went down,

he came to a good place to camp.

Jacob found a stone

to use for a pillow.

Then he lay down to sleep.

Jacob dreamed of a tall stairway.

The stairway went all the way

from earth to heaven.

Jacob saw angels of God

going up and down the stairway.

God stood at the top of the stairs

and spoke to Jacob.

God said, "I am the Lord,

God of your grandfather, Abraham,

and the God of your father, Isaac.

The ground you are lying on

belongs to you.

Your family will cover the land.

Everyone will be blessed

through your family.

I will be with you and protect you

wherever you go.

Someday I will bring you back here.

I will give you everything

I have promised."

God can be trusted to keep his promise.
Hebrews 10:23, NLT

The next morning Jacob got up early.

He took the stone that was his pillow

and stood it up to be a marker.

Jacob made a promise.

"I want God to be with me

and protect me on this journey.

I want God to bring me back safely.

If he does, I will make him my God."

Story based on Genesis 28:10-22 as it appears in the New Living Translation®.

Joseph's brothers are jealous
Genesis 37:1-36

Jacob loved his son Joseph.

Jacob gave Joseph a special gift—

a beautiful robe.

Joseph's brothers hated Joseph.

They could not say kind words to him.

One night Joseph had a dream.

He told his brothers about his dream.

"Listen to this dream," Joseph said.

"We were tying up bundles of grain.

My bundle stood up,

and your bundles bowed low to it!"

His brothers hated him even more

because of Joseph's dream.

Soon after this happened, Jacob said,

"Joseph, go see how your brothers

and the sheep are getting along."

Joseph's brothers saw him coming.

"Let's kill that dreamer!" they said.

"We can say a wild animal ate him.

Then we'll see if his dreams are true!"

But one brother said,

"Let's not kill him.

Let's throw him into this pit."

When Joseph came,

they pulled off his beautiful robe

and threw Joseph into the pit.

Love is not jealous or boastful or proud.
1 Corinthians 13:4, NLT

When some traders on camels came by,

the brothers sold Joseph to be a slave.

Then they dipped his robe in blood

and took it to Jacob.

When Jacob saw the robe, he said,

"A wild animal has eaten him!"

Jacob was sad for a long time.

No one could make him feel better.

Story based on Genesis 37:1-36 as it appears in the New Living Translation®.

Joseph forgives
Genesis 42:1-16; 43:8, 9, 15; 45:3-15

No food was growing in Jacob's land.

Jacob sent his sons to Egypt for food.

But Benjamin, Jacob's youngest son,

was not allowed to go.

Joseph was governor over all of Egypt.

He was in charge of selling the food.

His brothers came and bowed to him.

"We come to buy food," they said.

Joseph's brothers did not know him,

but Joseph knew who they were.

Joseph pretended to be a stranger.

He remembered his old dreams.

Joseph said to them, "You are spies!"

"No!" they said. "We just want food.

We are brothers, not spies!

Our father lives in Canaan.

Our youngest brother is with him."

Joseph said, "I will test your story.

You must go and get your brother.

I will keep one of you here in prison."

When the brothers told Jacob,

their father was very afraid.

Judah promised to care for Benjamin.

When they returned, Joseph was glad.

"I am Joseph!" he said to his brothers.

His brothers could not believe it!

The Lord forgave you, so you must forgive others.
Colossians 3:13, NLT

"You sold me as a slave," Joseph said.

"But it was God who sent me here.

For seven years no food will grow.

God sent me to Egypt

to keep you and your families alive.

And he has made me the king's friend.

Bring my father to me quickly.

Tell him everything you have seen."

Story based on Genesis 42:1-16; 43:8, 9, 15; 45:3-15 as it appears in the New Living Translation®.

God keeps Moses safe
Exodus 1:22-2:10

God's people, the Hebrews,

lived in the land of Egypt.

Pharaoh, the king, was afraid of them,

so he made the Hebrews his slaves.

Then Pharaoh said,

"Kill all the baby Hebrew boys."

One Hebrew woman had a baby boy.

He was a beautiful baby.

The mother hid him for three months.

Then she got a basket made of reeds.

She made it so water could not get in.

The mother put her baby in the basket

and laid the basket at the river's edge.

The baby's sister waited nearby
to see what would happen.
Soon Pharaoh's daughter came.
When the princess saw the basket,
she opened it.
The princess found the baby boy.
His crying made her want to help.
"He must be a Hebrew boy," she said.
The baby's sister spoke
to the princess.
"Shall I find someone
to care for the baby?" she asked.
"Yes, do!" said the princess.

He [God] will take care of you.
Psalm 55:22, NLT

The girl brought her mother
to the princess.

"I will pay you for help,"
the princess said.

So the mother took her baby home
and cared for him until he was older.

Then the princess adopted the boy.

She named her new son Moses.

Story based on Exodus 1:22–2:10 as it appears in the New Living Translation®.

God calls Moses to help
Exodus 3:1-14

While Moses was

taking care of sheep,

he went out

into the wilderness.

Moses was near the mountain of God.

Suddenly, Moses saw

the angel of the Lord,

who looked like fire in a bush.

The bush was filled with flames,

but it did not burn up.

"Amazing!" Moses said.

"Why isn't that bush burning up?

I must go over to see this."

"Moses!" God called from the bush.

"Here I am!" Moses said.

"Do not come any closer," God said.

"Take off your sandals.

This is holy ground.

I am the God of Abraham,

of Isaac, and of Jacob."

Moses hid his face in his hands.

He was afraid to look at God.

God said, "I know my people,

the Hebrews, are slaves.

I will rescue them

and give them their own land.

You [God] heard their cries for help and saved them.
Psalm 22:5, NLT

"Now go. I am sending you
to Pharaoh, the king of Egypt.
You will lead my people out of Egypt."
Moses asked, "How can I lead them?"
God said, "I will be with you."
Still, Moses complained.
"They will ask, 'Who sent you?'"
God said, "Tell them I AM sent you."

Story based on Exodus 3:1-14 as it appears in the New Living Translation®.

The people cross the Red Sea

Exodus 14:5-31

Pharaoh, the king of Egypt,

let God's people, the Israelites, leave.

But then he changed his mind.

"Why did we let them go?" he asked.

Pharaoh decided to chase them

with all his troops and chariots.

The Israelites were camping

by the Red Sea.

When they saw Pharaoh's army,

they were afraid

and asked God for help.

Then they complained to Moses,

"Why did you make us leave Egypt?"

Moses said, "Do not be afraid.

Just watch God rescue you."

A pillar of cloud moved behind them,

so Pharaoh's army

could not see the Israelites.

Then God told Moses,

"Hold your staff out over the water."

When Moses raised his staff,

the waters parted.

The Israelites walked through the sea

on dry land!

The Egyptians followed them,

but God made their chariots break.

God will rescue his people.
Zechariah 9:16, NLT

"Let's get away!" the Egyptians yelled.

"God is fighting for Israel!"

After the Israelites made it across,

God told Moses,

"Raise your staff again."

The waters roared back into place,

and covered Pharaoh's whole army.

That is how God saved Israel that day.

Story based on Exodus 14:5-31 as it appears in the New Living Translation®.

God gives his laws
Exodus 19:1-20:21

The Israelites came to Mount Sinai.

Then Moses climbed the mountain

to meet with God.

God said, "Tell this to my people.

'You saw how I saved you from Egypt.

Now if you obey me,

you will be my special treasure.'"

Moses told the leaders what God said.

"We will do all that God says,"

the leaders of the people agreed.

God told Moses,

"I will come in a cloud

and speak so the people can hear me."

Then Moses told the Israelites,

"Get ready for an important event."

Three days later

there was a great thunderstorm.

A thick cloud covered Mount Sinai.

Then they heard a loud horn blast.

Moses led the people out

to meet with God.

They stood at the foot of the mountain

while it shook.

Then God told Moses

to climb to the top of the mountain.

There, God gave Moses his laws.

> **So be careful to obey my [God's] laws.**
> Leviticus 18:30, NLT

"Do not worship any other gods.

Do not make idols of any kind.

Do not misuse the name of God.

Rest on the seventh day. Keep it holy.

Honor your father and mother.

Do not murder. Respect marriage.

Do not steal. Do not lie.

Do not long for other people's things."

Story based on Exodus 19:1–20:21 as it appears in the New Living Translation®.

Exploring the new land

God told Moses, "Send out
twelve men to explore the new land
that I am giving you."
So Moses sent out twelve men.
Caleb, Joshua, and ten others went.
Moses told the men, "Go north.
See what the land is like.
Find out what the people are like."
The twelve men explored the land.
When they came back, they said,
"The land is good!
But the people there are powerful,
and the cities have strong walls."

64

"Let's go take the land!" Caleb said.

But the other men said, "We can't!

The people are like giants!

They are stronger than we are."

The Israelites cried and complained,

"Let's go back to Egypt."

Joshua and Caleb were very upset.

They said, "God will give us this land!

Do not disobey God! Do not be afraid!"

God appeared and spoke to Moses.

"Will these people ever believe in me?

I will destroy them

and make a new nation!"

> **I [God] will guide you along the best pathway.**
> Psalm 32:8, NLT

Moses said, "Please forgive them!

Show everyone how good you are."

God said, "I will forgive them.

But none of them will enter the land.

Only Caleb and Joshua can enter.

All the people must go back.

You will stay in the wilderness

and wander for forty years."

Story based on Numbers 13:1–14:35 as it appears in the New Living Translation®.

Rahab helps two spies
Joshua 2:1-24

Joshua sent two spies to Jericho.

They spent the night

at Rahab's house.

Someone told the king of Jericho,

so he sent a message to Rahab.

It said, "Bring out those spies."

"They were here, but they left,"

said Rahab. "Hurry!

You can probably catch them."

So the men went to find the spies.

Rahab went up to the roof.

She had hidden the two spies there,

under piles of flax.

Then Rahab talked with the spies.

"I know God gave you this land.

Everyone is afraid of you.

We have heard all God has done.

Your God is God of heaven and earth.

Promise to help me and my family.

When Jericho is captured, let us live."

The two spies agreed.

Then Rahab said, "Hide in the hills."

So the spies told Rahab,

"Hang up this red rope.

Keep all your family inside the house.

Everyone in the house will be safe."

Do not withhold good from those who deserve it.
Proverbs 3:27, NLT

Rahab hung the rope in the window,
and the spies went into the hills.
The king's men finally stopped
searching for the spies.
Then the spies went back to the camp.
"God will certainly give us the land.
All the people are afraid of us,"
the spies told Joshua.

Story based on Joshua 2:1-24 as it appears in the New Living Translation®.

Joshua captures Jericho
Joshua 6:1-23

Jericho's gates were shut tight

because the people were afraid

of the Israelites.

God told Joshua,

"I have given you Jericho.

Your army is to march around the city

every day for six days.

On the seventh day,

march around the city seven times.

Then the priests must blow horns.

Have the people give a mighty shout.

Then the walls of the city will fall."

So Joshua told everyone what to do.

The seven priests started marching.

Guards marched in front and in back.

"Do not shout or even talk,"

Joshua ordered.

They did this for six days.

On the seventh day,

the Israelites got up early

and marched around the city.

Finally, during the seventh time,

the priests blew their horns.

Joshua ordered the people, "Shout!

For God has given you the city!

But do not hurt Rahab or her family."

He [God] will give you victory!
Deuteronomy 20:4, NLT

They shouted as loud as they could.

Suddenly, the walls of Jericho fell.

The Israelites went in from every side
and captured Jericho.

The spies kept their promise to Rahab.

They brought Rahab and her family
out of her house
and took them to a safe place.

Story based on Joshua 6:1-23 as it appears in the New Living Translation®.

Deborah leads a battle
Judges 4:1-24

The Israelites had disobeyed God.

So God gave control of them

to the king of the Canaanites.

The commander of Jabin's army,

Sisera, was mean to the Israelites.

The Israelites cried to God for help.

Deborah was a prophet and judge.

She helped people

with their problems.

One day she sent for Barak.

She told Barak,

"God says, 'Go fight Sisera.

I will give you victory over him.'"

Barak said, "I will go,

but only if you go with me!"

"I will go with you," said Deborah.

But because you would not fight alone,

God's victory will be won

by a woman."

Barak called ten thousand warriors.

Deborah also marched with them.

Deborah told Barak, "Get ready!

God will give you victory over Sisera."

So Barak led his warriors into battle.

God threw Sisera's men into a panic.

Sisera jumped off his chariot and ran.

Be brave and courageous.
Psalm 27:14, NLT

Sisera ran to Jael's tent and said,

"Do not tell anyone I am here."

Sisera was so tired he fell asleep.

Jael quietly crept up to him.

Then she killed him

with a hammer and tent peg.

When Barak came,

he saw that Sisera was dead.

Story based on Judges 4:1-24 as it appears in the New Living Translation.

Gideon fights the Midianites
Judges 7:1-25

God told Gideon to rescue

the Israelites from the Midianites.

But God told Gideon,

"You have too many warriors.

When you win the battle,

they will think they did not need me.

Tell whoever is afraid to go home."

So many of the soldiers went home.

God said, "There are still too many!

Bring your men to a stream."

Only the three hundred who drank

water from their hands got to stay.

God said, "These men can fight."

One night God told Gideon, "Get up!
If you are afraid to attack,
go see the Midianite camp now.
Listen to what the Midianites say."
There were many Midianite soldiers.
One said, "I dreamed of a loaf of bread
that tumbled into camp
and knocked a tent over."
Another Midianite said,
"That must mean Gideon will win!"
Gideon thanked God for those words.
Gideon returned to his camp. "Get up!
God will help us beat the Midianites!"

For the LORD your God fights for you.
Joshua 23:10, NLT

When they reached the Midianites,

the men blew horns and broke jars.

Their torches blazed

and the soldiers yelled,

"For the Lord and for Gideon!"

Then the soldiers stood and watched

as the Midianites ran around shouting

and fighting one another!

Story based on Judges 7:1-25 as it appears in the New Living Translation®.

Delilah tricks Samson
Judges 16:4-31

Samson was a judge in Israel

when the Philistines ruled the land.

Samson was very, very strong.

After Samson fell in love with Delilah,

the Philistines went to see her.

The Philistines told her,

"Find out how we can tie him up."

So Delilah said to Samson,

"Please tell me why you are strong."

"If I am tied up with new bowstrings,"

Samson told her,

"I will be just like anyone else."

So she tied Samson up while he slept.

The Philistines tried to catch Samson,
but he snapped the bowstrings.
Delilah kept asking Samson his secret.
Finally Samson gave in.
"My hair has never been cut," he said.
"If my hair is cut, I won't be strong."
Delilah called the Philistines.
That night while Samson slept,
Delilah had someone shave off
all of Samson's hair.
The Philistines captured him
and gouged out his eyes.
Then they put Samson in prison.

You [God] are my strength.
Psalm 18:1, NLT

One day the Philistines had a party.

They brought Samson out to perform.

By that time, his hair was long again.

Samson prayed,

"God, please make me strong again."

Samson pushed on two pillars

with all his might.

The temple crashed down on them all.

Story based on Judges 16:4-31 as it appears in the New Living Translation®.

Ruth cares for Naomi
Ruth 1:1-2:23; 4:9, 10, 17

There was no food in Judah,

so Elimelech took his family to Moab.

He lived with his wife, Naomi,

and their two sons.

Then Elimelech died.

The sons married Orpah and Ruth.

When her sons died,

Naomi wanted to go home.

She heard there was food in Judah.

Naomi told Orpah and Ruth,

"Go back to your families."

Orpah wanted to stay in Moab.

But Ruth wanted to go with Naomi.

Ruth said, "I will stay with you,
and your God will be my God."
So Naomi and Ruth left.
In Bethlehem the grain was ready.
Ruth said, "Let me go into the fields
and gather the leftover grain."
Ruth gathered grain in Boaz's field.
Boaz was one of Naomi's relatives!
He saw Ruth working very hard.
Boaz found out she was his relative,
and he told Ruth, "Come to my fields.
Gather with the women in my fields.
"I will take care of you.

Be kind to each other.
Ephesians 4:32, NLT

"I know how you stayed with Naomi,
and how kind you have been.
May God bless you
since you trust him."
Boaz married Ruth
and took Naomi into his house.
Boaz and Ruth had a baby, Obed.
He became King David's grandfather.

Story based on Ruth 1:1–2:23; 4:9, 10, 17 as it appears in the New Living Translation®.

God speaks to Samuel
1 Samuel 3:1-21

Samuel worked in the temple with Eli

when messages from God were rare.

One night Eli had just gone to bed,

but Samuel was already asleep.

God called, "Samuel! Samuel!"

So Samuel ran to Eli and said,

"Here I am. What do you need?"

Eli told Samuel, "I did not call.

Go back to bed."

Samuel went back to bed,

but it happened again.

Now Samuel did not yet know God.

He did not know it was God calling.

God called Samuel a third time,

and Samuel jumped up and ran to Eli.

Then Eli knew God had called Samuel.

So Eli told Samuel, "Go and lie down.

If someone calls you, say, 'Yes, Lord.

Your servant is listening.'"

Samuel went back to bed.

God called again, "Samuel! Samuel!"

This time Samuel was ready and said,

"Yes, Lord. Your servant is listening."

God said, "I will punish Eli like I said.

His sons are doing wrong,

and Eli has not stopped them."

> **Listen closely to . . . everything I [God] say.**
> *Deuteronomy 6:3, NLT*

Samuel was afraid to tell Eli
what God said, but Eli asked him,
"What did God say?
Do not hide anything from me."
So Samuel told him everything.
All the people of Israel
knew Samuel was God's prophet,
because he told them God's words.

Story based on 1 Samuel 3:1-21 as it appears in the New Living Translation®.

God chooses David
1 Samuel 16:1-13

Saul was Israel's first king,

but he disobeyed God.

So God wanted to choose a new king.

God told Samuel,

"You have been sad long enough.

I have rejected Saul as king of Israel.

Fill your horn with oil.

In Bethlehem you will find Jesse.

One of his sons will be the new king."

Samuel did as God told him.

When Bethlehem's leaders saw him,

they were afraid and asked Samuel,

"Do you come in peace?"

"I have come to worship God.

Come with me," said Samuel.

Samuel invited Jesse and his sons, too.

When Samuel saw Jesse's son Eliab,

he thought, "He must be the king!"

But God said, "Do not judge by looks.

God does not decide the way you do!

People judge by how others look.

But God looks at a person's thoughts."

Jesse showed Samuel seven sons,

but Samuel said,

"None of these is God's chosen.

Are these all of your sons?"

God knows all hearts.
Proverbs 24:12, NLT

"There is one more," Jesse said.

"The youngest is watching the sheep."

"Send for him at once," Samuel said.

When David arrived, God said,

"This is the one. He will be the king."

So Samuel poured oil on David's head,

and God's Spirit came on David

from that day on.

Story based on 1 Samuel 16:1-13 as it appears in the New Living Translation®.

David wins a "giant" battle
1 Samuel 17:4-11, 32-51

There was a giant named Goliath

who wanted to fight the Israelites.

None of the soldiers would fight him,

so David said, "I will fight this giant!"

King Saul said, "Do not be silly!

You are only a boy,

and Goliath is a champion fighter!"

But David replied,

"I protect lambs from wild animals.

I have killed lions and bears,

and I will kill this Philistine, too.

He has made fun of the living God!

God will save me from him!"

Saul finally said, "All right.
May God be with you!"
Saul gave David his armor to wear,
but it was too big so David took it off.
David chose five smooth stones.
Then he took his staff and sling
and went to fight Goliath.
Goliath roared at David,
"You think you'll kill me with a stick?
Come here, and I will leave you dead!"
David shouted, "You have weapons,
but God Almighty is on my side!
It is his battle. He will give you to us!"

You [God] protect me from trouble.
Psalm 32:7, NLT

Goliath started to attack,

so David ran to meet him.

David hurled a stone using his sling.

The stone hit Goliath and he fell.

Then David used Goliath's sword

to cut off the giant's head.

When the Philistines saw this,

they ran away.

Story based on 1 Samuel 17:4-11, 32 51 as it appears in the New Living Translation®.

David finds a friend
1 Samuel 18:1-4; 20:1-42

David met Jonathan, King Saul's son,
and they became best friends.

But King Saul was afraid of David
and planned to have David killed.

David heard this and asked Jonathan,
"Why does Saul want to kill me?"

Jonathan said, "He will not kill you.
He would have told me."

David said, "Saul knows we're friends.
He would not tell you about his plan,
but I am sure he wants to kill me.
I usually eat with Saul on holidays,
but tomorrow I will hide in the field.

"Tell Saul I went to see my family.
If he says, 'Fine!' everything is OK.
But if he gets mad,
we will know he wants to kill me."
Jonathan promised to help and said,
"I will go to the field after we eat.
I will shoot arrows at the stone pile,
and then I will send a boy to get them.
If I say, 'They're on this side,' it is OK.
But if I say, 'Go farther,' leave!"
The next day Saul sat down to eat.
Saul asked, "Why isn't David here?"
Jonathan said, "He is with his family."

A friend is always loyal.
Proverbs 17:17, NLT

Saul became very angry and yelled,

"Go get David so I can kill him!"

So Jonathan went to the field.

He shot arrows and sent the boy out.

Jonathan called out, "Go farther!

Hurry! Do not wait!"

Then the boy left, and David came out.

David and Jonathan said goodbye.

Story based on 1 Samuel 18:1-4; 20:1-42 as it appears in the New Living Translation®.

David treats Saul kindly
1 Samuel 24:1-22

Saul's army was searching for David.

Saul went into a cave,

but David's men were hiding there!

"This is your chance!"

David's men whispered.

"God promised you power over Saul.

This must be what he meant."

So David crawled forward,

and cut off a piece of Saul's robe.

But David began to feel bad about it.

He said, "I should not have done it.

This is serious to attack God's king."

David did not let his men kill Saul.

After Saul left the cave,

David came out and shouted,

"My lord the king!"

When Saul looked at him,

David bowed down and said,

"Now you see I will not harm you.

Look at what I have in my hand—

a piece of your robe!

I cut it off, but I did not kill you

even though you are trying to kill me.

God will decide between us.

He might punish you,

but I will not harm you."

Love your enemies!
Matthew 5:44, NLT

Saul said, "Is that really you, David?"

Then Saul began to cry.

Saul said to David,

"You are better than I.

You were so kind to me today

when you did not kill me.

Now I know you will be king,

and you will make Israel great."

Story based on 1 Samuel 24:1-22 as it appears in the New Living Translation®.

David becomes king
2 Samuel 5:1-5; 7:8-16

The leaders of Israel

went to talk to David.

They said to him,

"We are all part of your family.

You have led us for a long time.

Even when Saul was king,

you were the real ruler.

The Lord has told you,

'You will lead Israel,

and you will shepherd my people.'"

So David promised to lead them.

They made David king of Israel

when he was thirty years old.

Then God spoke to Nathan

and told him to go to David and say,

"I chose you when you were a boy.

You were tending sheep in the field.

I have always been with you,

and I have destroyed all your enemies.

Now I will make you famous!

I have given this land to my people.

This land will always be theirs,

and it will be a safe place for them.

I will make your children kings!

One of your sons will be the next king.

I will make his kingdom strong.

You will be the shepherd of my people Israel.
1 Chronicles 11:2, NLT

"Your son will build a temple
for my name,
and his kingdom will last forever.
I will be his father,
and he will be my son.
If he sins, I will punish him.
But I will love him forever.
Your kingdom will last forever."

Story based on 2 Samuel 5:1–5; 7:8-16 as it appears in the New Living Translation®.

David shows kindness
2 Samuel 9:1-13

King David wanted to know

if anyone in Saul's family was alive.

David had promised Jonathan

to be kind to his family.

David asked Ziba,

one of Saul's old servants,

"Is anyone from Saul's family alive?

I want to show him God's kindness."

Ziba told King David,

"One of Jonathan's sons is alive,

but he is crippled."

David sent for Jonathan's son.

His name was Mephibosheth.

Mephibosheth came to see David.

He was very afraid of King David.

He said, "I am your servant."

But David said, "Do not be afraid!

I want to be kind to you,

because I promised your father.

I'll give you the land that was Saul's.

You may live in the palace with me!"

Mephibosheth was amazed

by David's kindness!

The king called Ziba and said,

"Mephibosheth will live here.

He will have everything that Saul had.

Show mercy and kindness to one another.
Zechariah 7:9, NLT

"Your family and your servants
will farm the land for Mephibosheth
and help produce food for his family."
Ziba replied, "I will do all you say."
From then on, Mephibosheth ate
with David and lived at the palace.
Mephibosheth became
like another son to David.

Story based on 2 Samuel 9:1-13 as it appears in the New Living Translation®.

Solomon asks for wisdom
1 Kings 3:1-28

King Solomon, David's son, loved God.

One night God spoke in a dream.

God asked him, "What do you want?

I will give you anything you ask for!"

Solomon replied to God,

"My father, David, was a great king.

Give me wisdom to rule your people."

God said, "You asked for a good gift.

I will give you what you asked for!

You will be the wisest man to live,

and I will give you riches and honor!"

Solomon awoke and went home.

He worshiped God with a big party.

One day two women came to the king

and asked Solomon

to settle their argument.

One said, "We both had babies.

This woman's son died in the night.

She took my son

and left me her dead baby.

But I know the dead baby's not mine."

The other woman said,

"The live baby is mine!"

They argued back and forth.

Finally Solomon said, "Bring a sword.

Each woman can have half."

Wisdom is better than silver . . . and gold.
Proverbs 3:14, NLT

One woman said,

"Give her the child! Do not kill him!"

The other woman said, "Divide him."

Then wise King Solomon said,

"Give him to the first woman.

She wants him to live,

because she is his true mother."

All were amazed by his wisdom.

Story based on 1 Kings 3:1-28 as it appears in the New Living Translation®.

The ravens feed Elijah
1 Kings 16:29-34; 17:1-7

King Ahab was the ruler of Israel,

but he was not a good king.

King Ahab did evil in God's sight.

Ahab did more evil things

than any other king

who ruled Israel.

Ahab worshiped false gods

and made the one true God angry.

God sent Elijah to talk to the king.

Elijah was one of God's prophets.

(A prophet is a person

who speaks God's words

to the people.)

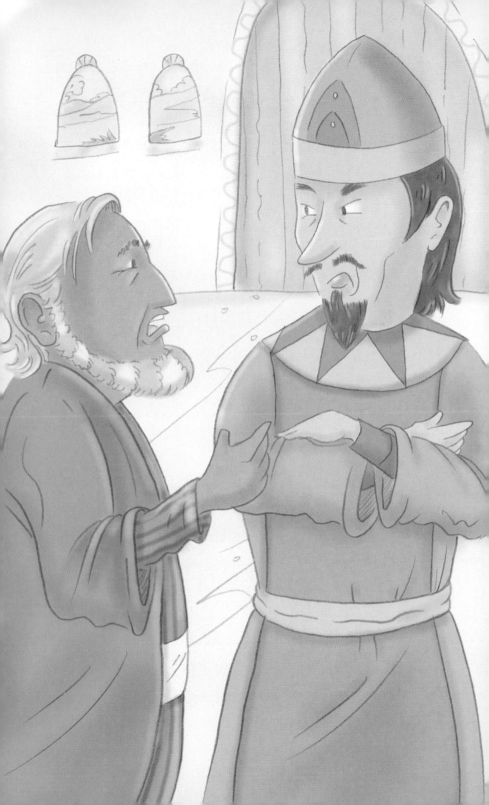

Elijah had a message from God
for King Ahab.

"There will be no dew or rain.

This will last for the next few years.

It will not rain again until I say so!"

Then God told Elijah, "Go east.

Hide by Kerith Brook
near the Jordan River.

Drink from the brook,
and eat what the ravens bring you.

I have ordered them to bring food."

Elijah did as God told him,
and God provided food and water.

He [God] fills the hungry with good things.
Psalm 107:9, NLT

Elijah camped beside Kerith Brook,

and the ravens brought

bread and meat.

They came each morning and evening.

Elijah drank from the brook,

but after a while the brook dried up.

There was no rainfall

anywhere in the land.

Story based on 1 Kings 16:29-34; 17:1-7 as it appears in the New Living Translation®.

Elijah helps a poor widow
1 Kings 17:8-24

God told Elijah, "Go to Zarephath.

A widow there will feed you."

When Elijah arrived in Zarephath,

he asked her for bread and water.

But the widow said,

"I have only a little flour and oil.

We will eat one last meal,

and then my son and I will die."

Elijah said, "Do not be afraid!

Go ahead and cook that 'last meal,'

but bake me a little loaf of bread first.

God will make the flour and oil last

until it rains again!"

The widow did as Elijah said.

They ate her flour and oil many days,

but there was always enough left.

It was just as God had promised.

Later, the woman's son became sick.

He grew worse until he died.

The widow said to Elijah,

"What have you done?

Did you kill my son to punish me

for the bad things I have done?"

Elijah replied, "Give me your son."

He laid the body on his bed and cried,

"God! Why did you let him die?"

He [God] gives breath and life to everyone.
Isaiah 42:5, NLT

Then Elijah stretched himself out
over the child three times.

He cried to God, "Let his life return!"

The Lord heard Elijah's prayer,
and the child came back to life!

"Look, your son is alive!" Elijah said.

The woman said, "Now I know that
you are a man of God."

Story based on 1 Kings 17:8-24 as it appears in the New Living Translation®.

Elijah battles Baal
1 Kings 18:16-40

King Ahab went out to meet Elijah.

Ahab said, "Here's the troublemaker."

Then Elijah said,

"You are Israel's troublemaker.

You have refused to obey God,

and you worship images of Baal.

Bring all the people and the prophets

of your gods to Mount Carmel."

When the people were gathered,

Elijah stood up and said,

"If the Lord is God, follow him!

But if Baal is God, follow him!"

But the people said nothing.

So Elijah said, "Prepare two sacrifices.

Put them on altars. Do not light them.

Call on your god. I'll call on the Lord.

The true God will light the fire!"

All the people agreed.

Baal's prophets called on Baal.

They danced wildly around their altar.

Elijah joked, "Shout louder.

Maybe he is asleep!"

Still Baal did not answer.

Then Elijah called, "Come over here!"

Elijah rebuilt God's altar

and piled wood and the sacrifice on it.

The LORD alone is God!
Joshua 22:22, NLT

Elijah told the people

to pour water on the altar.

Then he prayed, "God, answer me.

Let the people know you are God."

Then fire flashed down from heaven.

It burned up the soggy sacrifice!

The people saw this, fell on their faces,

and cried, "The Lord is God!"

Story based on 1 Kings 18:16-40 as it appears in the New Living Translation®.

Elijah goes to heaven
2 Kings 2:1-15

God was about to

take Elijah up to heaven.

Elijah and Elisha were traveling,

when Elijah said to Elisha, "Stay here.

God has told me to go to Bethel."

But Elisha said, "I'll never leave you!"

So they went on together to Bethel.

The prophets from Bethel asked,

"Elisha, did you know

God is taking your master away?"

"Quiet!" Elisha answered. "I know."

Then Elijah said to Elisha, "Stay here.

God has told me to go to Jericho."

Elisha would not leave Elijah.

Finally they stopped by the river.

Elijah folded up his cloak.

Then the river parted

and they went across on dry ground!

On the other side, Elijah asked Elisha,

"What can I do for you before I go?"

Elisha said, "Let me take your place."

"That is a difficult thing," Elijah said,

"but if you see me when I go, you can.

If you do not see me, you cannot."

Suddenly a chariot of fire appeared.

A whirlwind carried Elijah to heaven.

Tell everyone about God's power.
Psalm 68:34, NLT

Elisha saw it and yelled, "My father!"

The chariot and Elijah disappeared.

Elisha picked up Elijah's cloak,

and he returned to the Jordan River.

Then Elisha struck the water

with the cloak.

The river divided,

and Elisha crossed over.

Story based on 2 Kings 2:1-15 as it appears in the New Living Translation®.

Elisha heals Naaman
2 Kings 5:1-19

The king of Aram liked Naaman.

Naaman was a mighty warrior.

But he had a very bad skin disease.

Naaman's wife had

a slave from Israel.

The slave girl said,

"My master should go to Samaria.

The prophet there could heal him."

When Naaman told the king,

the king said, "Go visit the prophet."

He sent a letter to the king of Israel.

The king said, "The people of Aram

just want to invade again!"

But Elisha said, "Send Naaman to me,
and he will find a true prophet here."
So Naaman went to Elisha's house,
and Elisha sent a message out to him.
The message said,
"Go to the Jordan River.
Wash seven times,
and then you will be healed."
But this made Naaman angry.
"I did not expect this!" he said.
"He did not come out to see me.
The Jordan is not even a good river."
But his officers said, "Just try it."

He [God] heals all my diseases.
Psalm 103:3, NLT

So Naaman went down to the Jordan
and dipped himself seven times.

His skin became healthy!

He was healed!

Then Naaman went to find Elisha.

Naaman said,

"Now I know God is the true God.

I will only worship him."

Story based on 2 Kings 5:1-19 as it appears in the New Living Translation®.

Jonah runs away
Jonah 1:1-3:3

God told Jonah, "Go to Nineveh!
Tell them I have seen
the bad things they do."
Jonah did not want to go,
so he got on the wrong ship.
He wanted to escape from God,
but God sent a powerful storm.
The ship was about to sink.
The men on the ship were praying
and throwing supplies overboard.
The men rolled dice
because they wanted to find out
who had made God angry.

When they rolled, Jonah lost.

They asked Jonah what he had done.

Jonah told them he ran from God.

"Throw me into the sea," Jonah said.

"Then the storm will calm down."

The sailors tried to row the boat,

but they could not make it to shore.

The sailors asked God to forgive them

and then threw Jonah into the sea.

The storm stopped at once!

Then the sailors worshiped God.

God sent a big fish to swallow Jonah.

Jonah was in the fish for three days.

Obey his [God's] commands.
Ecclesiastes 12:13, NLT

While Jonah was inside the fish,

he prayed to God.

Jonah said, "Only God can save me."

God told the fish to spit Jonah out.

Then God told Jonah again,

"Go to Nineveh, and give the people

the message I gave you."

This time Jonah obeyed.

Story based on Jonah 1:1–3:3 as it appears in the New Living Translation®.

King Josiah finds God's Word
2 Kings 22:1–23:3

Josiah was a good king

who always did what pleased God.

When King Josiah was twenty-six,

he wanted to fix the temple.

The people gave gifts

to pay for the repairs.

Hilkiah, the high priest,

counted the money in the temple.

While Hilkiah worked,

he discovered a scroll and said,

"I have found God's Law!"

Hilkiah sent a man named Shaphan

to read the scroll to Josiah.

When the king heard what was
written, he tore his clothes in despair.
King Josiah gave orders
to Hilkiah and Shaphan.
"Go to the temple,
and speak to God for us all.
Ask about the words in this scroll.
The Lord must be very angry with us
because we have disobeyed the Law."
The men went to the prophet Huldah.
She told them, "God is very angry.
He will destroy this city and its people
just as he said in the scroll.

All those who love me [Jesus] will do what I say.
John 14:23, NLT

"But God heard how Josiah wants
to obey, so he will not destroy Judah
while Josiah is alive."
They took her message back to Josiah.
He called everyone to the temple,
and read the whole Law to them.
King Josiah pledged to obey the Lord,
and all the people followed Josiah.

Story based on 2 Kings 22:1–23:3 as it appears in the New Living Translation®.

Daniel chooses to obey
Daniel 1:1-21

King Nebuchadnezzar
captured Jerusalem
and took treasures from the temple.
He also captured some young men
and took them back to Babylon.
Nebuchadnezzar told his helper,
"Select strong, healthy young men
who are wise and have good sense."
The king wanted these men
to be his new royal advisers.
The men would train for three years
and learn how Babylonians live.
Daniel and three friends were chosen.

They had the best food and wine,

but they did not want to eat it.

Daniel asked for other food

because it was against God's rules.

The guard said,

"You will become pale and thin.

Then I will get in trouble."

So Daniel told the guard,

"Let us eat vegetables and drink water

for ten days, and see how we look."

When the ten days passed,

Daniel and his friends

looked better than all the others.

We must obey God rather than human authority.
Acts 5:29, NLT

When the test was over,

they did not eat the king's food again.

God made Daniel and his friends

excellent learners.

God also gave Daniel a special ability,

so he could understand dreams.

The four friends were the wisest people

in the kingdom.

Story based on Daniel 1:1-21 as it appears in the New Living Translation®.

The fiery furnace
Daniel 3:1-30

King Nebuchadnezzar made a statue
and told all the people to come see it.
The king's messenger shouted,
"Listen! When you hear the music,
you must bow and worship the statue,
or you will go in the fiery furnace."
The instruments started to play,
and the people bowed to worship.
Some of the king's wise men said,
"Shadrach, Meshach, and Abednego
will not bow."
Then Nebuchadnezzar told them,
"You get one more chance to bow.

"If you do not, you'll go to the furnace.

What god can save you then?"

They replied, "Our God can save us,

but even if he doesn't, we won't bow."

Nebuchadnezzar became very angry.

The king had the three friends tied up.

Then strong men threw

the three friends into the furnace.

It was so hot the strong men died!

Suddenly Nebuchadnezzar jumped up.

The king asked,

"Didn't we throw three men in?

Now I see four men in the fire.

God rescues the godly from danger.
Proverbs 11:8, NLT

"They are not even hurt by the flames,
and the fourth man looks like a god!"
Then the king shouted,
"Shadrach, Meshach, Abednego!
Come out!"
The three men stepped out of the fire.
Then King Nebuchadnezzar said,
"Their God rescued them!"

Story based on Daniel 3:1-30 as it appears in the New Living Translation®.

The writing on the wall
Daniel 5:1-31

King Belshazzar gave a great party.
The king and his guests drank
from cups stolen from the temple
and made toasts to honor their idols.
Right then, a human hand appeared
and began writing on the palace wall.
The king's face turned pale with fear.
Then he shouted to the magicians,
"Tell me what this writing means."
But none of them could read it,
so they were very afraid.
The king's mother said,
"Send for Daniel because he is wise."

Daniel was brought before the king.

The king told him,

"I have heard of your wisdom.

My wise men cannot read this writing.

If you read it, you will be honored."

Daniel answered, "I do not want gifts,

but I'll tell you what the writing says.

Remember your father?

King Nebuchadnezzar was too proud.

He went crazy and lost everything

because he didn't learn that God rules.

You knew about this, Belshazzar,

but you have not honored God.

The kings of the earth belong to God.
Psalm 47:9, NLT

"You used God's cups from the temple, and you have praised idols.

The writing says:

'Mene, mene, tekel, parsin.'

It means God is ending your reign because you have failed the test.

Your kingdom will be divided."

That very night, the king was killed.

Story based on Daniel 5:1-31 as it appears in the New Living Translation®.

Daniel in the lions' den
Daniel 6:1-28

King Darius made Daniel powerful
and the other officials were jealous.
They wanted to get Daniel in trouble,
but he never did anything wrong.
"We will use his faith in God
to trick him."
So the officials told the king,
"We think you should make a law
that people can only pray to you.
If they pray to anyone else,
you will throw them to the lions."
King Darius signed the law.
Daniel went home and prayed to God.

The officials saw Daniel praying
and went to tell the king.
They said, "Daniel still prays to God.
He pays no attention to your law."
The king was angry he made the law.
He tried to find a way to save Daniel,
but the officials said,
"You know the rules.
No law signed by you can be changed."
At last, the king had Daniel arrested
and thrown into the lions' den.
The king said, "May God save you."
He worried about Daniel all night.

Day by day the LORD takes care of the innocent.
Psalm 37:18, NLT

In the morning King Darius
rushed to the lions' den and asked,
"Daniel, did God rescue you?"
Daniel answered, "Long live the king!
God protected me from the lions."
Darius ordered that Daniel be let out
and the officials be put in the den.
Darius praised God for saving Daniel.

Story based on Daniel 6:1-28 as it appears in the New Living Translation®.

Queen Esther saves God's people
Esther 2:16-20; 4:7-5:3; 7:1-10

King Xerxes loved Esther

and made her his queen.

Esther was Jewish,

but she kept it secret from Xerxes.

The king appointed a new official,

whose name was Haman.

Haman was the most powerful official.

All the other officials bowed to him.

But Mordecai, Esther's uncle,

refused to bow down to Haman

because Mordecai worshiped only God.

When Haman found this out,

he was angry.

When he learned Mordecai was a Jew,

Haman said, "There are people

who do not obey the laws of the king.

These people should be destroyed."

The king agreed to the plan.

Mordecai and the Jews were sad.

So Mordecai told Esther,

"You must go and talk to the king,

and ask him to save your people.

God made you queen

for a time like this."

Going to see the king was dangerous,

but Esther decided she must.

God in heaven appoints each person's work.
John 3:27, NLT

The king told Queen Esther,

"Tell me what you want."

Esther replied, "Please spare my life.

My people and I will be killed."

"Who would touch you?" he asked.

Esther said, "Haman is our enemy."

King Xerxes stopped the plan.

He sentenced Haman to death instead.

*Story based on Esther 2:16-20; 4:7–5:3; 7:1-10 as it appears in the New
Living Translation®.*

An angel visits Zechariah
Luke 1:5-25, 57-64

Zechariah was a Jewish priest
who served God in the temple.
He and his wife, Elizabeth,
were very old and had no children.
One day Zechariah was serving
at the altar of incense
when an angel appeared to him.
The angel said, "Do not be afraid!
God has heard your prayer,
and your wife will have a son!
You are to name him John.
John will be filled with the Spirit
and prepare people for God's coming."

Then Zechariah asked the angel,
"How can I know this will happen?"
So the angel replied, "I am Gabriel!
God sent me to tell you
this good news!
You did not believe what I said,
so now you will not be able to speak
until John's birth.
For my words will come true."
When Zechariah left, he couldn't talk.
Soon, Elizabeth found out
that she was going to have a baby.
She was very happy at God's kindness.

It is impossible to please God without faith.
Hebrews 11:6, NLT

Elizabeth had a baby boy.

The relatives wanted

to name him Zechariah.

But Elizabeth said,

"No! His name is John!"

Zechariah wrote, "His name is John!"

Then Zechariah could speak again,

and he began praising God!

Story based on Luke 1:5-25, 57-64 as it appears in the New Living Translation®.

The Savior is born
Luke 2:1-20

The Roman emperor wanted a census

to count the people in the empire.

Joseph had to go to Bethlehem,

so he took Mary with him.

It was almost time for Mary's baby.

While Mary and Joseph

were in Bethlehem,

she gave birth to her first child, a son.

She wrapped him in strips of cloth

and laid him in a manger

because there was no room in the inn.

That same night shepherds guarded

their sheep in the fields.

An angel of the Lord appeared.

The Lord's glory surrounded them,

and the shepherds were very afraid.

But the angel said, "Do not be afraid!

I have good news of joy for everyone!

The Savior is born in Bethlehem!

This is how you will recognize him.

You will find a baby in a manger.

He will be wrapped in strips of cloth!"

Suddenly, more angels appeared.

The angels were praising God:

"Glory to God in highest heaven,

Peace on earth to all God favors."

The Savior . . . has been born tonight in Bethlehem!
Luke 2:11, NLT

When the angels returned to heaven,

the shepherds said, "Let's go

and see the great thing God told us!"

So the shepherds ran to Bethlehem

and found Mary, Joseph, and the baby.

After the shepherds saw Jesus,

they told everyone what happened.

Everyone who heard was amazed.

Story based on Luke 2:1-20 as it appears in the New Living Translation®.

The wise men visit Jesus
Matthew 2:1-12

Jesus was born in Bethlehem

at the time when King Herod ruled.

Some wise men came

to Jerusalem and asked,

"Where is the newborn king?

We have seen his star as it rose,

and we have come to worship him."

Herod was very upset

by their question.

King Herod called a meeting

of the Jewish leaders and asked,

"Where did the prophet say

this baby will be born?"

The Jewish leaders said,

"This is what the prophet wrote:

'O Bethlehem of Judah,

You are not just a small village,

for a ruler will come from you.

He will shepherd my people.'"

So Herod sent a message

and asked the wise men to see him.

Herod asked them about the star.

Then he told them, "Go to Bethlehem.

Search carefully for the child.

When you find him, come tell me,

so I can go worship him, too!"

All kings will bow before him [God].
Psalm 72:11, NLT

After the meeting the wise men left,
and the star guided them to the child.
The wise men entered the house.
They fell down and worshiped Jesus
and gave him gifts.
When they left, they found a new way
because God had warned them
not to return to Herod.

Story based on Matthew 2:1-12 as it appears in the New Living Translation®.

Young Jesus teaches in the temple
Luke 2:41-52

Every year Jesus' family went
to Jerusalem to celebrate Passover.
One year when the festival ended,
the family started the journey home.
Jesus stayed behind in Jerusalem,
but he did not tell anyone.
Mary and Joseph did not miss him
because at first they thought
he was with friends.
But when Jesus did not show up later,
they started to look for him.
They could not find him with anyone,
so they returned to Jerusalem.

They were worried

because Jesus was only twelve.

Three days later they found Jesus.

He was in the temple with teachers.

They were asking difficult questions.

Everyone was amazed by Jesus.

Mary and Joseph were confused.

Jesus' mother said to him, "Son!

Why have you done this to us?

Your father and I have been worried.

We searched for you everywhere."

Jesus said, "Why did you search?

Of course I am in my Father's house."

Honor your father and mother.
Ephesians 6:2, NLT

But his parents did not understand
what he meant.

Jesus returned to Nazareth
and obeyed Mary and Joseph.

Jesus grew both in height
and in wisdom.

He was loved by God
and all who knew him.

Story based on Luke 2:41-52 as it appears in the New Living Translation®.

John baptizes Jesus
Mark 1:1-11

Isaiah was a prophet of God

who shared God's messages.

One message Isaiah shared was:

"I send a messenger before you.

He will prepare your way.

He is a voice in the wilderness.

He shouts, 'Prepare a pathway

for the Lord!

Make a straight road for him!'"

This messenger was John the Baptist.

John lived in the wilderness

and told people to turn away from sin

and be baptized.

People from all over

went to see and hear John.

They asked God

to forgive their sins,

and then John baptized them.

John's clothes were woven camel hair

and he wore a leather belt.

He ate locusts and wild honey.

John said, "Someone great is coming!

I am not good enough to be his slave.

I baptize you with water,

but he will baptize you

with the Holy Spirit!"

You [John] will prepare the way for the LORD.
Luke 1:76, NLT

One day Jesus came from Nazareth,

and asked John to baptize him.

When Jesus came up out of the water,

Jesus saw the heavens open.

The Spirit landed on him like a dove,

and a voice came from heaven.

It said, "You are my beloved Son.

I am fully pleased with you."

Story based on Mark 1:1-11 as it appears in the New Living Translation®.

Jesus faces temptation
Luke 4:1-13

When Jesus left the Jordan River,

he was filled with the Holy Spirit.

The Spirit led him to the wilderness,

where the Devil tempted Jesus.

Jesus ate nothing for forty days,

so he was very hungry.

The Devil said,

"If you are God's Son,

turn this stone into bread."

But Jesus told him, "No!

The Scriptures say,

'Bread is not enough.

People need more than that for life.'"

Then the Devil showed him the world.

Jesus saw every kingdom at one time.

The Devil told Jesus,

"I can give this to anyone.

I will give it to you if you worship me."

But Jesus said, "The Scriptures say:

'Worship only the Lord your God.'"

So the Devil took Jesus to Jerusalem

to the highest point of the temple.

The Devil said, "Jump off!

The Scriptures say, 'Angels guard you.

They will hold you with their hands.

Your foot will not hit a stone.'"

Don't let us yield to temptation.
Luke 11:4, NLT

Then Jesus replied,

"The Scriptures also say this:

'Do not test the Lord your God.'"

When the Devil

was finished tempting Jesus,

he left Jesus

until the next opportunity came.

Story based on Luke 4:1-13 as it appears in the New Living Translation®.

Jesus calls the disciples
Luke 5:1-11

One day Jesus was preaching
on the shore of the Sea of Galilee.
There were huge crowds
because many people wanted
to hear God's Word.
Jesus saw two boats by the water
that the fishermen had left there.
While the fishermen
were washing their nets,
Jesus stepped into Simon's boat.
Jesus asked Simon
to push it into the water.
Jesus taught from the boat.

After teaching, Jesus spoke to Simon.

"Now go out where it is deeper.

Let down your nets,

and you will catch many fish."

Simon said, "We worked all night.

We did not catch anything.

But if you say so, we will try again."

So the fishermen let down their nets,

and the nets became so full

that they began to rip!

They called their partners to help.

Soon both boats were so full of fish

that they were about to sink.

Jesus [said], "Follow me."
John 21:19, NLT

Simon fell to his knees before Jesus.

Simon said, "Lord, please leave me.

I am too much of a sinner!"

All of the fishermen were amazed.

Jesus said to Simon, "Do not be afraid!

Now you will be fishing for people!"

The fishermen left everything

and followed Jesus.

Story based on Luke 5:1-11 as it appears in the New Living Translation®.

Jesus heals a paralyzed man
Mark 2:1-12

Jesus traveled to Capernaum.

People came to where Jesus stayed.

The house became packed with people,

and there was not even room

for one more person.

Jesus preached God's Word to them.

There were four men

who tried to get through the crowd.

They wanted Jesus

to see their friend who could not walk.

The friends could not

get near Jesus in the crowd,

so they dug through the roof.

The four men lowered the sick man
through the hole.
They put him right in front of Jesus.
Jesus saw their faith
and spoke to the sick man.
Jesus said, "Your sins are forgiven."
Some teachers of the law heard Jesus.
The teachers thought, "This is wicked!
Who but God can forgive sins?"
Jesus knew what they were thinking,
and said to them,
"Why is this wickedness?
I will prove that I can forgive sins."

I am the LORD who heals you.
Exodus 15:26, NLT

Jesus turned to the sick man and said,

"Stand up and take your mat home.

You are healed!"

The man jumped up and took the mat.

He pushed through

the surprised crowd of people.

Everyone praised God saying,

"We've never seen anything like this!"

Story based on Mark 2:1-12 as it appears in the New Living Translation®.

Jesus teaches about prayer
Matthew 6:5-15

Jesus taught his disciples

about prayer.

He told them,

"When you pray,

do not be like the pretenders.

They love to pray

so everyone can see them,

but that is all the reward

they will ever get.

When you pray, go away by yourself.

Shut the door behind you.

Pray to your Father in secret

and talk to God like you know him.

"The pretenders repeat their words,

but your Father knows what you need.

This is how you should pray:

'Our Father in heaven,

may your name be honored.

May your Kingdom come soon.

May your will be done here on earth,

just as it is in heaven.

Give us our food for today,

and forgive us our sins,

just as we have forgiven others.

Do not let us yield to temptation.

Deliver us from the evil one.'"

Pray at all times.
Ephesians 6:18, NLT

Then Jesus taught this lesson

about forgiveness:

"If you forgive others,

God will forgive you.

But if you refuse

to forgive others,

your Father will not

forgive your sins."

Story based on Matthew 6:5-15 as it appears in the New Living Translation®.

Jesus calms a storm
Mark 4:35-41

Jesus was with his disciples at sunset.

He said to them,

"Let's cross the lake."

They were already in the boat,

so they started to cross

to the other side of the lake.

Jesus and the disciples

left the crowds behind,

but some people in boats

followed them.

Soon a fierce storm arose.

High waves came into the boat

until it was nearly full of water.

While all this was happening,
Jesus was sleeping in the boat
with his head on a cushion.
The disciples were very afraid,
so they woke Jesus up and shouted,
"Teacher, don't you care
that we are going to drown?"
When Jesus woke up,
he scolded the wind.
Then he said to the water,
"Quiet down!"
Suddenly the wind stopped,
and there was a great calm.

Don't be troubled or afraid.
John 14:27, NLT

Jesus asked his disciples,

"Why are you so afraid?

Do you still not have faith in me?"

They were filled with awe.

Then the disciples asked each other,

"Who is this man?

Even the wind and waves obey him."

Story based on Mark 4:35-41 as it appears in the New Living Translation®.

Jesus feeds the five thousand
John 6:1-14

A big crowd followed Jesus around
because they saw his miracles.
Jesus went up into the hills
to spend some time with his disciples.
He sat down with his disciples,
but Jesus soon saw a crowd.
The people were looking for him.
Jesus asked Philip,
"Where can we find food
to feed all of these people?"
Jesus was testing Philip.
Philip told Jesus,
"Feeding them would cost a lot!"

Andrew, Simon Peter's brother, said,

"There is a boy here with some food.

He has five loaves and two fish.

But how can that help this crowd?"

Jesus told his disciples,

"Tell everyone to sit down."

So all of them sat down on the grass.

There were over five thousand people.

Then Jesus took the loaves and fish

and thanked God.

He passed them out

to the people,

and they all ate until they were full.

God will generously provide all you need.
2 Corinthians 9:8, NLT

Then Jesus said,

"Pick up the leftovers.

Do not let anything be wasted."

There were twelve

baskets of leftovers!

The people were amazed

at this miracle and said,

"He is the Prophet we've waited for!"

Story based on John 6:1-14 as it appears in the New Living Translation®.

Jesus walks on water
Matthew 14:22-33

Jesus sent his disciples to the boat,
and they crossed the lake.
Then Jesus sent the huge crowd home
and went off by himself to pray.
Night fell while he was alone.
The disciples were in trouble.
There was a strong wind
and they were fighting big waves.
Very early in the morning Jesus came
to them, walking on the water.
When the disciples saw him,
they screamed because they thought
he was a ghost.

Jesus spoke to them at once.

"It is all right. I am here!"

Jesus said, "Do not be afraid."

Peter called to him, "Lord!

If it is you, let me come to you.

Let me walk on the water."

Jesus said, "All right, come."

Peter went over the side of the boat

and walked toward Jesus.

When Peter looked around

at the high waves,

he got very scared and began sinking.

Peter shouted, "Save me, Lord!"

Do not be afraid. I [the Lord] am here to help you.
Isaiah 41:13, NLT

Jesus reached out and grabbed him.

Jesus told Peter,

"You do not have much faith.

Why did you doubt me?"

They climbed back in the boat.

Then the wind stopped,

and the disciples worshiped him.

"You really are the Son of God!"

Story based on Matthew 14:22-33 as it appears in the New Living Translation®.

The good Samaritan
Luke 10:25-37

An expert in law wanted to test Jesus,

so the expert asked Jesus,

"How can I get eternal life?"

Then Jesus asked him,

"What does the law of Moses say?"

The man replied, "'You must love God

with your heart,

soul, strength, and mind.'

And 'Love your neighbor as yourself.'"

Jesus said, "Do this and you will live!"

The man wanted to feel good,

so he asked, "Who is my neighbor?"

Jesus answered by telling a story:

"A Jewish man was on a trip.

He was attacked by bandits.

The bandits robbed him, beat him up,

and left him half dead beside the road.

A Jewish priest came along

and saw the man lying there.

He passed by on the other side.

Then a temple assistant did the same.

Finally, a Samaritan came along.

When he saw the man,

the Samaritan felt sorry for him.

The Samaritan kneeled down

and treated the Jewish man's wounds.

Love your neighbor as yourself.
Matthew 19:19, NLT

"The Samaritan took the man
to an inn and took care of him.
The next day the Samaritan gave
the innkeeper money and asked him
to take care of the wounded man."
Jesus asked, "Who was the neighbor?"
The man said, "The one who helped."
Jesus said, "Yes. Now do the same."

Story based on Luke 10:25-37 as it appears in the New Living Translation®.

The lost son returns
Luke 15:11-32

Jesus told this story

about God's love for sinners.

"A man had two sons.

The younger son spoke to his father

and said, 'I do not want to wait.

I want my share of your wealth now.'

So his father agreed

and divided his wealth.

The younger son traveled far away.

He wasted all his money,

and he began to starve.

A local farmer hired him to feed pigs,

but no one gave him anything to eat.

"When the pigs' food looked good,

he thought, 'I am dying of hunger.

I will go home and say,

"Father, I have sinned.

I do not deserve to be your son.

Please take me on as a servant."'

So he returned home to his father.

When his father saw him,

the father ran to hug and kiss him.

His son said what he had planned,

but his father told the servants,

'Bring him a robe, sandals, and a ring!

We must have a big party.'

God is love.
1 John 4:16, NLT

"The older son was working in a field.

He returned home to the party.

A servant said, 'Your brother is home!'

The older brother was angry,

but his father said,

'You are always with me.

Your brother was lost,

but now he is found!'"

Story based on Luke 15:11-32 as it appears in the New Living Translation®.

Mary makes a wise choice
Luke 10:38-42

Jesus and his disciples

were going to Jerusalem.

While they were traveling,

he and his disciples

came to a village.

A woman named Martha

welcomed them into her home.

Her sister, Mary,

sat at the Lord's feet

and listened

to what Jesus taught.

But Martha did not sit

and listen to Jesus.

Martha was too busy worrying

about the big dinner

that she was working hard to make.

Martha came to Jesus and said,

"It is not fair.

My sister is just sitting here,

while I am doing all the work!

Tell Mary to come

and help me."

But Jesus said to her,

"My dear Martha,

you are upset

about all these little things!

Make the Kingdom of God your primary concern.
Matthew 6:33, NLT

"There is really
only one important thing
that you should care about.
Mary has discovered it—
and I will not take it
away from her."

Story based on Luke 10:38-42 as it appears in the New Living Translation®.

Jesus welcomes the children
Mark 10:13-16

One day some parents

decided to bring their children

to see Jesus.

The parents wanted Jesus

to touch their children

and bless them.

But the disciples

told the parents,

"Do not bother Jesus."

When Jesus saw

what was happening,

he was very unhappy

with his disciples.

Jesus told his disciples,

"Let the children

come to me.

Do not stop them!

God's Kingdom is for children

and for people

who have faith like children.

This is the right kind of faith.

I promise you

that only the people

who have faith like this

will be part of

the Kingdom of God."

Let the children come to me [Jesus].
Mark 10:14, NLT

Then Jesus took the children
into his arms.
He put his hands
on their heads
and blessed them.

Story based on Mark 10:13-16 as it appears in the New Living Translation®.

Jesus heals Bartimaeus
Mark 10:46-52

When Jesus and his disciples
were leaving Jericho,
a crowd of people followed them.
A blind beggar named Bartimaeus
sat by the road.
Bartimaeus heard
that Jesus was nearby.
He started to shout,
"Jesus, Son of David, help me!"
Some of the people yelled at him
and told him, "Be quiet!"
Bartimaeus shouted louder,
"Son of David, help me!"

When Jesus heard Bartimaeus,

he stopped walking.

Jesus told the people,

"Tell him to come here."

So the crowd called to

the blind man.

The people told Bartimaeus,

"Cheer up.

Come on, Jesus is calling you!"

Bartimaeus jumped up

and came to Jesus.

Jesus asked Bartimaeus,

"What do you want me to do?"

The LORD hears his people.
Psalm 34:17, NLT

The man who was blind said,

"I want to see!"

Jesus said to Bartimaeus,

"Go on your way.

Your faith has healed you."

Right then, the blind man could see!

Then Bartimaeus followed Jesus

down the road.

Story based on Mark 10:46-52 as it appears in the New Living Translation®.

Jesus and Zacchaeus
Luke 19:1-10

Jesus was going through Jericho.

There was a man named Zacchaeus

who lived in Jericho.

Zacchaeus helped

the Romans collect taxes.

He was one of the most powerful Jews,

and he had become very rich.

Zacchaeus tried to get a look at Jesus

as Jesus walked by.

But Zacchaeus was too short to see

above the crowds of people.

So he climbed a tree beside the road

and watched from up there.

When Jesus came by,

he looked up at Zacchaeus.

Jesus said,

"Zacchaeus! Quick, come down!

I need to visit your home today."

Zacchaeus climbed

down the tree quickly.

He was happy

to take Jesus to his house.

But the people

were not happy.

They complained and said,

"Jesus is visiting a sinner."

In . . . Jesus there is forgiveness for your sins.
Acts 13:38, NLT

Zacchaeus talked to Jesus.

Zacchaeus even promised,

"I'll give half of my money to the poor.

If I have taken too many taxes,

I will give back four times as much!"

Jesus said, "Salvation has come here.

This man has shown he is a true Jew.

I came to save lost people like him."

Story based on Luke 19:1-10 as it appears in the New Living Translation®.

The people praise Jesus
Matthew 21:1-11

Jesus and the disciples

were near Jerusalem.

Jesus sent two disciples ahead.

Jesus told the two disciples,

"Go into the village over there.

You'll see a donkey and its colt there.

Untie them and bring them here.

If anyone asks what you are doing,

just say, 'The Lord needs them.'"

This was done as the prophets said.

"Look, your King is coming to you.

He does not show off.

He rides on a donkey's colt."

The two disciples did what Jesus said.
The disciples brought the donkey
and its colt to Jesus.
Then they threw some clothing
over the colt, and Jesus sat on it.
Many people spread coats on the road.
Others cut branches from the trees
and spread the branches on the road.
Jesus was the center of the parade.
The crowds all around him shouted,
"Thank God for the Son of David!
Bless the one who comes
in the name of God!"

Everyone will praise him [God]!
Isaiah 61:11, NLT

The whole city noticed
and was stirred up
when Jesus entered Jerusalem.
"Who is this?" they asked.
The crowds replied, "It is Jesus.
He is the prophet
who comes from Nazareth."

Story based on Matthew 21:1-11 as it appears in the New Living Translation®.

Jesus washes the disciples' feet
John 13:1-15

It was almost time

for the Passover celebration.

Jesus knew God had given him power,

and he knew he had come from God.

Jesus knew he would return to God.

He wanted to show the disciples love.

So when it was time for supper,

Jesus got up from the table.

Then he took off his robe

and wrapped a towel around his waist.

Jesus poured water into a basin

and began to wash the disciples' feet.

He wiped them with his towel.

When Jesus came to Peter,

Peter asked him,

"Why are you washing my feet?"

Jesus told him,

"You do not understand now,

but someday you will understand."

Peter said in protest, "No!

You will never wash my feet!"

Jesus told Peter,

"If I do not wash you,

you will not belong to me."

When he finished,

Jesus put on his robe again.

Follow God's example in everything you do.
Ephesians 5:1, NLT

Jesus sat down and said,

"Do you understand what I was doing?

You call me 'Teacher' and 'Lord.'

You are right, because it is true.

I, Lord and Teacher, washed your feet.

You ought to wash each other's feet.

I have given you an example to follow.

Do as I have done to you."

Story based on John 13:1-15 as it appears in the New Living Translation®.

Jesus' trial and death
Luke 23:1-27

Jewish leaders took Jesus to Pilate.

They said, "This man causes trouble.

He tells people not to pay taxes

and says he is the Messiah, a king."

Pilate asked Jesus,

"Are you King of the Jews?"

Jesus replied, "Yes, it is as you say."

Pilate told the priests and the crowd,

"I find nothing wrong!"

But the crowd was unhappy,

so Pilate sent Jesus to Herod.

Herod was happy to see Jesus

because he wanted miracles.

Herod asked Jesus many questions,

but Jesus refused to answer.

Herod and his soldiers

made fun of Jesus

and put a royal robe on him.

Then they sent him back to Pilate.

Pilate called everyone together saying,

"You say this man causes trouble,

but I find him innocent.

Herod also thinks he is innocent.

Jesus does not deserve to die.

I will have him beaten and released."

But the crowd shouted, "Kill him!"

He [Jesus] died for our sins.
Galatians 1:4, NLT

The crowd wanted Pilate

to release a different man.

Pilate argued with them,

but they kept shouting, "Kill him!"

Pilate gave Jesus to the crowd.

They led Jesus away to die on a cross.

Crowds followed him. Many cried.

Story based on Luke 23:1-27 as it appears in the New Living Translation®.

Jesus is alive!
Luke 24:1-12

Very early on Sunday morning,

some women came to Jesus' tomb.

They were bringing spices

for Jesus' body.

When they arrived at the tomb,

they saw that the stone

covering the entrance

had been rolled away.

The women went inside the tomb,

but Jesus' body was not there!

They tried to figure out

what had happened

to Jesus' body.

Suddenly, two men appeared

wearing shining robes.

The women were very afraid,

so they bowed low before the men.

The men said,

"People who are alive aren't in tombs.

Jesus is not here!

He has risen from the dead!

Don't you remember what he said?

Jesus said he would die on a cross.

But he also told you

that he would rise again

on the third day."

Christ died and rose again.
Romans 14:9, NLT

Then the women remembered,

and they rushed

to tell everyone what happened.

The disciples did not believe them,

but Peter went to the tomb to look.

He saw the empty wrappings

that had covered Jesus.

Peter left, confused.

Story based on Luke 24:1-12 as it appears in the New Living Translation®.

The walk to Emmaus
Luke 24:13-34

Two of Jesus' followers
were walking to Emmaus.
They were talking
about the things that happened.
Suddenly, Jesus began walking
on the road with them,
but the men didn't know it was Jesus.
Jesus said, "You seem to be upset.
What are you talking about?"
One man said, "Haven't you heard?
So much has happened in Jerusalem."
Jesus asked, "What happened?"
So the two men told him everything.

"Jesus was a prophet and teacher,

and we thought he was the Messiah.

But some temple leaders killed him.

That all happened three days ago.

But this morning,

some women went to his tomb.

They saw angels who said,

'Jesus is alive!'

Some of our men ran out to see, and,

sure enough, Jesus' body was gone."

Jesus told them, "You foolish people!

That was all in the Scriptures."

Then Jesus explained the Scriptures.

Look, I [Jesus] am alive forever and ever!
Revelation 1:18, NLT

Then the men ate with Jesus.

Jesus blessed some bread.

Then he broke it and gave it to them.

Suddenly, they saw that it was Jesus!

Right then he disappeared!

The men went to the other disciples
and heard more news:

"Jesus is really alive! Peter saw him!"

Story based on Luke 24:13-34 as it appears in the New Living Translation®.

Jesus appears to Thomas
John 20:19-31

Jesus had been
with his disciples in the room
and had shown them his scars.
When Jesus breathed on
the disciples who were there,
they received the Holy Spirit.
But Thomas was not with them
when Jesus came.
The other disciples told him,
"We have seen Jesus!"
But Thomas said, "I won't believe,
not until I touch the wounds
in his hands and in his side."

The next week

the disciples were together again.

This time Thomas was with them.

The doors were locked.

Just as before,

Jesus suddenly appeared in the room.

Jesus said to them,

"Peace be with you."

Then Jesus said to Thomas,

"Touch my hands.

Touch the wound in my side.

Do not be filled with doubt. Believe!"

Thomas said, "My Lord and my God!"

All who believe in him [Jesus] have eternal life.
John 3:36, NLT

Then Jesus told him,

"You saw me and believed.

The blessed ones

believe without seeing."

Some of Jesus' miracles are written

so everyone can believe.

All who believe in Jesus

will live forever.

Story based on John 20:19-31 as it appears in the New Living Translation®.

Jesus appears to his friends
John 21:1-14

Later Jesus came back

to the disciples.

Peter and several other disciples

were near the Sea of Galilee.

Peter told them,

"I am going fishing."

The other disciples decided

they would go too.

So they all went out in the boat.

They did not catch any fish all night.

At dawn the disciples

saw Jesus on the beach,

but they could not tell who he was.

Jesus called out, "Friends,
have you caught any fish?"
The disciples told him, "No."
Jesus said, "Throw your net
on the right side."
So they did what Jesus told them.
There were so many fish in the net,
they couldn't pull the net in the boat!
One disciple said, "It is the Lord!"
Then Peter jumped in the water
and swam to the shore.
The others stayed with the boat
and pulled the loaded net to shore.

We have seen his [Jesus'] majestic splendor.
2 Peter 1:16, NLT

When they got there,

a fire was burning, fish were frying,

and there was bread.

Jesus told them,

"Bring some of your fish."

So Peter went and got the net.

Then Jesus said,

"Now come and eat breakfast!"

Story based on John 21:1-14 as it appears in the New Living Translation®.

Jesus returns to heaven
Acts 1:3-14

Jesus appeared to his disciples

many times after the crucifixion.

Jesus wanted the disciples to be sure

that he was really alive.

When they were together,

Jesus told the disciples

about God's Kingdom.

One time when they were eating,

Jesus told the disciples,

"Do not leave Jerusalem

until God sends

what he promised.

I have told you about this before.

"John baptized with water.

You will be baptized with the Spirit."

The disciples often asked Jesus,

"When will Israel be free again?"

Jesus said, "Only God knows the time.

It is not for you to know.

But the Holy Spirit will come on you,

and you will receive power.

Tell people everywhere about me."

After Jesus said this,

he went up into the sky.

The disciples watched

as Jesus disappeared into a cloud.

Yes, I [Jesus] am coming soon!
Revelation 22:20, NLT

They kept looking until two men

in white robes suddenly appeared.

The two men said,

"Why are you staring at the sky?

Jesus has been taken into heaven.

Someday he'll return the same way!"

So the disciples returned to Jerusalem

and kept meeting together to pray.

Story based on Acts 1:3-14 as it appears in the New Living Translation®.

The Holy Spirit comes
Acts 2:1-42

Seven weeks after Jesus arose,

the believers were all meeting.

Suddenly, they heard a mighty wind

that filled the house where they were.

They saw what looked like flames

settle on each of their heads.

All of the believers

were filled with the Holy Spirit.

Then they began speaking

in other languages

through the power of the Spirit.

Crowds of people came running

to see what was happening.

The Jews from other nations
were absolutely amazed.
They asked, "How can this be?
These people are all from Galilee,
but they are speaking our languages!
They are telling great things of God!"
So Peter stepped forward and said,
"God proved that Jesus was his Son,
but you killed God's Son on a cross.
Then God raised him from the dead,
and we all saw it!
Now Jesus is in heaven, and God
sent his Spirit as he promised."

God has sent the Spirit of his Son into your hearts.
Galatians 4:6, NLT

Then the people asked the apostles,

"What should we do?"

So Peter told them,

"Repent and be baptized.

Then you will receive the Holy Spirit."

Many people believed

and were baptized.

Three thousand joined the church.

Story based on Acts 2:1-42 as it appears in the New Living Translation®.

Saul on the road to Damascus
Acts 9:1-25

Saul wanted to arrest Jesus' followers,

and he was on the way

to Damascus to find them.

Saul saw a bright light from heaven!

He fell to the ground

and heard a voice saying, "Saul! Saul!

Why are you hurting me?"

"Who are you, sir?" Saul asked.

The voice said, "I am Jesus.

Now get up and go to Damascus."

The men with Saul were surprised.

They heard a voice but saw no one!

When Saul got up, he was blind.

Saul's friends took him to Damascus.

The Lord spoke in a vision

to a believer named Ananias.

He said, "Go to Judas's house.

When you arrive, ask for Saul.

I told Saul that you will heal his eyes."

Ananias said, "But Lord!

I've heard the bad things Saul does."

God said, "Go and do what I say.

Saul will bring my message to many."

So Ananias went and did as God said.

Ananias put his hands on Saul's eyes,

and Saul could see!

Christ Jesus came into the world to save sinners.
1 Timothy 1:15, NLT

Saul stayed in Damascus to preach.

Everyone who heard him was amazed.

They knew Saul had come

to capture believers,

but now Saul preached about Jesus

as the Messiah!

The Jewish leaders wanted to kill him,

but some believers helped Saul escape.

Story based on Acts 9:1-25 as it appears in the New Living Translation®.

Peter visits Cornelius
Acts 10:1-48

Cornelius believed in God of Israel,

but he was not Jewish.

God gave Cornelius a vision.

An angel of God said, "Cornelius!

God has noticed

your prayers and gifts.

Send some men to Joppa to get Peter.

Ask Peter to come and visit you."

Cornelius obeyed the angel.

God also gave Peter a vision.

Peter saw a sheet come from the sky.

The sheet was filled

with many kinds of animals.

God said, "Kill and eat the animals.

If I say it is OK, it is OK."

Peter had the same vision three times.

Then the men Cornelius sent arrived.

The men asked for Peter at the gate.

The Spirit told Peter,

"I sent these men."

So Peter went down and said,

"I am Peter. Why have you come?"

The men said,

"An angel told Cornelius

to invite you to talk to him."

So Peter went with the men.

Go and make disciples of all the nations.
Matthew 28:19, NLT

When they arrived,

Cornelius told Peter about his vision.

Peter realized God talks to everyone,

not only to Jews.

Peter told Cornelius all about Jesus,

and everyone who listened believed.

The Holy Spirit fell on them, too,

and they were all baptized.

Story based on Acts 10:1-48 as it appears in the New Living Translation®.

Peter escapes from prison
Acts 12:1-17

King Herod began to hurt believers.

James was killed with a sword.

Then the king had Peter arrested.

The church was praying for Peter

while he was in prison.

The night before Peter's trial,

he was asleep in his cell.

Sixteen soldiers guarded Peter.

Suddenly an angel of God came.

The angel tapped Peter to wake him.

Then the angel said, "Quick! Get up!"

The chains fell off Peter's wrists.

"Get dressed and follow me!"

Peter left and followed the angel,

but he thought he was only dreaming.

They left the prison,

and then the angel suddenly left him.

Peter finally saw what had happened.

"It is really true!" he said to himself.

"The Lord sent an angel to save me!"

He knocked at the door in the gate

at the home where the people prayed.

A servant girl named Rhoda

came to open it.

But Rhoda was so happy

that she forgot to open the door!

You [God] faithfully answer our prayers.
Psalm 65:5, NLT

Rhoda ran back inside

to tell everyone Peter was there.

But no one believed Rhoda.

Finally they went to the door.

They were amazed to find Peter there!

He told them to quiet down.

Then Peter told them

how God had led him out of jail.

Story based on Acts 12:1-17 as it appears in the New Living Translation®.

Paul and Silas in prison
Acts 16:16-34

Paul, who used to be called Saul,

and Silas went to Philippi.

They were preaching about Jesus.

While they were in Philippi,

some people became angry.

The people did not like the things

that Paul and Silas were teaching.

The people told the authorities,

"Paul and Silas break the rules!"

So the authorities beat Paul and Silas

and threw them into prison.

Paul and Silas prayed and sang to God

while the other prisoners listened.

Suddenly, there was an earthquake.

The doors of the prison opened!

Every prisoner's chains fell off!

When the jailer woke up,

he saw that the doors were wide open.

The jailer was afraid that

the prisoners had all escaped.

The jailer was about to kill himself,

but Paul shouted,

"Stop! We are all here!"

The jailer fell down before them.

Then he asked Paul and Silas,

"What must I do to be saved?"

The Lord knows how to rescue godly people.
2 Peter 2:9, NLT

Paul and Silas replied,

"Believe in the Lord Jesus!

Then you will be saved."

Paul and Silas told

the jailer's whole family about Jesus.

Everyone believed and was baptized.

The jailer and his whole family

rejoiced because they believed in God.

Story based on Acts 16:16-34 as it appears in the New Living Translation®.

Paul's nephew helps him
Acts 23:12-35

A group of forty Jews pledged

not to eat until Paul was killed.

They told the priests and leaders:

"We will not eat until Paul is dead.

You should tell the commander

to make Paul go back to the council.

Say you want to hear his case again.

Then we will kill him

while he is on the way."

Paul's nephew heard this plan.

He went to the prison and told Paul.

Then Paul sent his nephew

to tell the commander.

The commander called two officers.

He ordered them,

"Get two hundred soldiers.

Have them ready at nine o'clock.

Also take two hundred spearmen

and seventy horsemen.

Get Paul safely to Governor Felix."

Then the commander wrote a letter:

"Greetings, Governor Felix!

This man was seized by some Jews

who were plotting to kill him.

I learned Paul is a Roman citizen,

so I moved him to safety.

> **A brother is born to help in time of need.**
> Proverbs 17:17, NLT

"The Jews argue with Paul over law,

but he has done nothing wrong.

When I heard of a plot to kill him,

I immediately sent him to you.

I have told the Jews to talk to you."

So the soldiers took Paul to Felix,

And Felix kept Paul safe

to wait for his accusers.

Story based on Acts 23:12-35 as it appears in the New Living Translation®.

Paul's ship is wrecked
Acts 27:1-44

Paul was on a boat

with some other prisoners.

An officer was taking them to Rome.

They stopped at many ports

because the weather was so bad.

Paul talked to the ship's workers

about not sailing in the winter.

But the sailors wanted

to get to a better harbor.

They thought they could do it,

so the sailors continued sailing.

But then a terrible storm

blew them off course.

Finally the sailors lost all hope.

But Paul told the crew,

"You should have listened to me.

But take courage! None of you will die!

The ship will go down, but you'll live.

An angel told me, 'Do not be afraid.

You will surely make it to Rome!

And God will keep everyone safe.'

Take courage! It will be as God said."

Then the sailors sensed land was near.

The water was not as deep as before,

and they were afraid to run into sand,

so they threw away the heavy anchors.

The LORD protects me from danger.
Psalm 27:1, NLT

When it was almost morning,

Paul begged everyone to eat.

Soon after that, they saw land.

The ship ran into the sand,

and it broke apart and sank.

The officer told everyone to get off.

They swam and floated ashore.

Everyone made it safely!

Story based on Acts 27:1-44 as it appears in the New Living Translation®.

John sees a vision of heaven
Revelation 21:1-27

John, the disciple, was very old.

He had been sent to live on an island.

While he was there,

God gave him a vision of the future.

This is what John saw:

"I saw a new heaven and a new earth.

The old heaven and earth

had disappeared.

And I saw the holy city,

the new Jerusalem.

It came down from God out of heaven.

Jerusalem looked

like a beautiful bride.

"I heard a loud shout from the throne:

'God lives with his people now!

He will take away their sadness.

There will be no more death.

There will be no more crying or pain.

The old world's problems are gone.'"

Jesus said, 'I make all things new!'

Jesus also said, 'It is finished!

I am the Beginning and the End.

My children will have these blessings.

But people who turn away will die.'

One of the angels said, 'Come!'

The angel showed me the holy city.

The Lord still rules from heaven.
Psalm 11:4, NLT

"Jerusalem was filled with God's glory.
It was made of sparkling jewels,
and the gates were made of pearls.
The streets were made of pure gold.
The glory of God will light the city,
and all nations will walk in its light.
No evil will be allowed to enter.
All who belong to Jesus can come."

Story based on Revelation 21:1-27 as it appears in the New Living Translation®.

Memory Verse Index

Here is a list of memory verses printed with each Bible story from the New Living Translation®.

309

THE NLT™ STORY BIBLE SERIES

Seven Books, Seven Reasons.

The **NLT**™ Story Bible Series is the easy choice. Here's why:

Reason 1 — It covers every age and stage of your child's development.

It grows with your child from birth to twelve. **Reason 2**

Reason 3 — The **NLT**™ is today's most popular new Bible version.

It's easy for your child to understand because the **NLT**™ is user-friendly. **Reason 4**

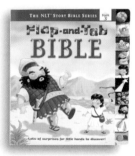

Reason 5 — It's easy for you to choose just the right book for your child.

It was developed with input from best-selling author and child development expert Dr. Mary Manz Simon. **Reason 6**

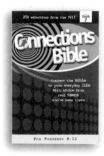

Reason 7 — It's published by Standard Publishing, the leader in children's Bible storybooks.

Word-and-Picture Bible
Item no: **04141**
ISBN: **0-7847-1594-7**

Touch-and-See Bible
Item no: **04142**
ISBN: **0-7847-1595-5**

Flap-and-Tab Bible
Item no: **04143**
ISBN: **0-7847-1596-3**

Play-and-Learn Bible
Item no: **04144**
ISBN: **0-7847-1597-1**

On-My-Own Reader Bible
Item no: **04145**
ISBN: **0-7847-1598-X**

One Way Bible
Item no: **04146**
ISBN: **0-7847-1599-8**

Connections Bible
Item no: **04147**
ISBN: **0-7847-1500-9**

Standard PUBLISHING
www.standardpub.com